POCKET CADDY

GOLF TIPS TO IMPROVE YOUR GAME

From The Editors Of

GOLF TIPS ® MAGAZINE

Sterling Publishing Co., Inc.
New York

Library of Congress Cataloging-in-Publication Data

Pocket caddy : golf tips to improve your game / from the editors of
Golf Tips® Magazine.
    p. cm.
  Includes index.
  ISBN 1-4027-1441-6
  1. Golf—Handbooks, manuals, etc. I. Golf Tips.
GV965.P595 2004
796.352—dc22

            2004010741

10 9 8 7 6 5 4 3 2

Published by Sterling Publishing Co., Inc.
387 Park Avenue South, New York, NY 10016
© 2004 by *Golf Tips® Magazine* editors
Distributed in Canada by Sterling Publishing
℅ Canadian Manda Group, 165 Dufferin Street
Toronto, Ontario, Canada M6K 3H6
Distributed in Great Britain by Chrysalis Books Group PLC
The Chrysalis Building, Bramley Road, London W10 6SP, England
Distributed in Australia by Capricorn Link (Australia) Pty. Ltd.
P.O. Box 704, Windsor, NSW 2756, Australia

Printed in China

Sterling ISBN 1-4027-1441-6

For information about custom editions, special sales, premium and
corporate purchases, please contact Sterling Special Sales
Department at 800-805-5489 or specialsales@sterlingpub.com.

*The golf instructions in the following pages were initially
featured in Golf Tips® Magazine, published by Werner
Publishing Corporation.*

Contents

Introduction

ince 1989, *Golf Tips® Magazine* has dedicated its pages to providing the game's most in-depth instruction. Often, this education has come in the form of a quick tip an instantly applicable lesson that serves to bandage a swing wound and could prevent your game from bleeding to death on a particular day. Most of our guidelines, however, are in the form of more extensive features that cover all aspects of golf, with a bent toward providing readers with what's necessary for lasting improvement.

It's our opinion that the key to real improvement is knowledge. In golf, as with most other facets of life, knowledge is king. Knowledge empowers the golfer to produce successful shots. It multiplies the number of plays a golfer can draw on to hit the ball high, low, to the left—or whatever the situation requires. More importantly, knowledge gives any golfer the ability to self-diagnose a problem. No one hits the ball perfectly every time, and this fact makes understanding why a golf ball behaves the way it does—and making the necessary adjustments—so critical to playing well, instead of just hoping for a better swing the next time around.

It's in the nature of learning that we learn best from repetition. All golfers want quick tips that can help them out on the course, but it's the slow and steady accumulation of experience through practice that makes a good habit stick. That's why we've divided this book into two parts: Drills and Fixes. The Drills are intended to address ongoing issues in your game, providing you with the knowledge and visual references you need to play your best tomorrow, next week, and for as long as you can walk and swing and put a ball on a tee. The Fixes are the quick solutions for problems that can derail a round, as well as creative approaches to tricky situations that can crop up in the course of play.

It would take you a lifetime to draw on the wisdom of all the teachers whose advice and aid are assembled in these pages. Read this book and carry it around with you so you can try out its advice: it will make you a smarter golfer and point the way to lasting improvement.

David Denunzio

DRILLS

Drive for Show

POWER DRILLS

All golfers want to hit the ball farther—it's only natural. There's something truly satisfying about swinging a club and watching the ball soar into the distance—and even more satisfying when that distance outdoes that of your partners.

Power isn't everything (accuracy is almost certainly more important), but that doesn't mean you should give up trying to achieve extra distance off the tee. These drills will help you develop your power potential, but without sacrificing the accuracy you need to hit the fairway with your longest drives.

Hear the Whoosh

Power derives from maximizing controlled velocity through the hitting zone. To develop an accurate sense of that acceleration, and to make sure it comes at the right time, hold your driver just under the clubhead and make a "whooshing" sound with the shaft. Swing the club about ankle-high and pay attention to where the "whoosh" occurs. It should be at the bottom of the swing.

Hinge and Load

You can't release the clubhead through impact if you haven't loaded it up in the first half of the swing with a proper wrist hinge. Build strength and learn what a proper wrist hinge feels like with this drill: Hold one or two golf clubs out in front of you, waist-high (**A**). Anchor your arms to your stomach and keep them there, isolating the motion to the wrists. Raise up the club or clubs, hinging your wrists (**B**). That hinged wrist is what you want to feel at the top of your backswing.

A   **B**

Shift Your Weight

Using your driver, make a baseball swing that emulates your favorite slugger. Make sure to swing the club on a level plane, not up and down. This drill improves weight transfer and promotes a more level swing and a better angle of attack—the sweeping motion you want from the tee. Swing at three different levels: ankle-high, knee-high, and waist-high.

Change Speeds

Take your driver and make swings at 50%, 75%, and 100% speed. Focus on keeping the arms and upper body

synchronized. Concentrate on the swing path and on releasing the clubhead. This drill promotes improved tempo and better ball contact.

Swing for the Fences

To hit big drives, you need to increase your clubhead speed. The key to generating as much speed as your body can muster is in delaying contact. All big hitters hang back on their right sides (if right-handed) and, more importantly, hit from there. At impact, you should still be able to see your back foot and feel your arms swinging away from you, to the target (**A**).

Hanging back at impact begins with the setup (**B**). Compare the two address positions here. In the first, long-drive competitor Patrick Dempsey has set up with his weight over his front foot. In his improved setup (**C**), the majority of his weight is distributed over his back foot—a solid position established by setting his right shoulder lower than the left and positioning his right elbow inside his left.

A   **B**   **C**

At the top of the swing, you want to feel your weight loaded over your right foot, with your left shoulder packed underneath your chin. By doing so, you'll not only store a tremendous amount of power but, if you stay on your right side for as long as possible as you swing the club back toward the ball, you'll give yourself more time to square the face. In **D**, Patrick's big shoulder turn may give the impression of a powerful top position, but he's failed to get his weight fully back on his right side. In **E**, Patrick, if asked to, could lift his left foot in his new top position. He's fully loaded, has kept a steady head, and has turned his left shoulder.

The true key to generating maximum power is to hit *from* the right side, not *with* the right side.

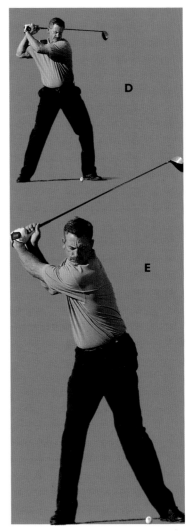

Lead with Your Left

When you want to get some extra distance out of your drives, it's natural to think that your right or dominant hand (for right-handed golfers) should supply the power. In reality, maximum power is the result of a left-hand lead.

The best way to feel the proper start of the downswing is to imagine that your right arm is being pulled by the left for as long as possible. A great drill to get used to this feeling is to release your right hand from the club at the start of your downswing, and to swing only with your left. With practice, this drill will lead to more power and control.

Left Shoulder Over Right Knee

The ability to hit powerful drives begins with the first move away from the ball. During the takeaway, most amateurs fail to turn appropriately and forget to shift their weight. If they turn, they forget to shift; if they shift, they forget to turn.

Think "left shoulder over right knee" on the takeaway. In other words, shift your weight and turn your shoulders until your left shoulder is positioned above your right knee. The right knee is a great benchmark for a solid upper-body rotation. Be careful not to overrotate your hips in order to get your right shoulder into position; instead, mini-mize hip movement to generate greater torsion.

Tension-Free Driving

When it comes to driving, one of the most common problems is carrying too much tension. Overly tense muscles not only rob you of distance, but make accurate driving (and long driving for that matter) extremely difficult. Tension also saps your body's energy, making it that much more difficult to play your best. And one of the most crucial and overlooked sources of harmful tension is gripping the club too tightly.

To find the right grip pressure, pick up your driver and grip it as hard as you can, taking a few practice swings. We'll call that pressure a 10. Now grip the club and swing it while holding it only with the thumb and forefingers of both hands. Consider that pressure a 1. Swinging the club with those four fingers not only reduces tension, but helps generate a feeling of effortlessness all the way through impact. Because you don't have enough strength with a four-finger grip to manipulate the club, this grip forces you to swing simply by turning back and using only your body's momentum and the force of gravity. After taking a number of swings in this manner, you should find that this feeling carries over into your regular swing, improving both your tempo and your timing.

Now use your normal grip, and concentrate on keeping the pressure at 4 or less. Once you've determined what the correct pressure feels like, make it your only goal during the swing to concentrate on maintaining that exact grip pressure from setup to finish. By concentrating solely on grip pressure, you should be better able to swing freely without worrying about other things. You'll also become more aware of what's going on with your body and your swing thanks to the lack of tightness in your hands and arms.

SLICE STOPPERS

Amateur golfers suffer more from slicing than from any other major swing flaw. It's very difficult to play well with a slice, as the uncontrollable curve has a way of causing the greatest trouble on the course. Throughout this section, we'll put special emphasis on the steps you can take to turn your high-arching shot shape into a more powerful, penetrating ballflight.

Step Back for an Inside Path

The most common fault that causes slicing is a swing path that goes from the outside in. To understand the feeling of swinging with a proper path, set up with your right foot pulled back. Your objective is to hit at a pronounced draw, starting to the right of the target and coming back to the left.

This drill ensures that you make the proper inside path. It also helps you recognize the way it should feel when your right hand and forearm cross over, and when releasing the clubhead—another must for stopping a slice and increasing power.

Keep Your Body Closed

Another common cause of slicing is a tendency to open the body too much at impact (**A**). This prevents you from squaring the clubface in time, as your lagging arms pull the club across the target line.

To eradicate this flaw, try the "parallel foot" drill. First assume your address position, and then turn your front toe back so it's pointing away from the target. Place the ball in line with the middle of your front foot and begin swinging slowly. Your body will feel closed, and it will be almost impossible to open it too quickly (**B**). You'll most likely begin hooking the ball because of your closed shoulder position. However, with regular practice, your tendency to slice should disappear for good.

A

B

Full-Swing Drills

FUNDAMENTALS OF ACCURACY

When you watch Tour pros on television, you probably notice their good tempo as well as their outstanding balance. But what's most striking is how effortless their swings appear to be, given the power and crispness they generate. Unlike most amateurs, the pros are always working on the most basic fundamentals of the swing. So, master these drills, and you'll be swinging and hitting like a pro.

Setup Keys

❶ To properly position your legs, begin by placing your feet just outside your hips, with your toes pointed outward at about 25 degrees. Then make sure your knees are relaxed and slightly bowed.

❷ It's crucial to position your upper left arm on top of your chest, not to the side of it. Allow your left arm to hang naturally, and slightly bend your right arm at the elbow.

❸ To promote a proper takeaway, the right shoulder must be slightly lower than the left at address.

❹ The clubshaft should be perpendicular to the ground and not forward pressed.

Takeaway

A solid takeaway is as important as any other aspect of the golf swing. The first step is the setup; the second is setting the swing on the right path from the start.

Grip a long iron just below the handle, and rest the butt of the club on your stomach. Elevate the shaft so the club-head is about at knee height, and concentrate on feeling that your torso, arms, hips, legs, and club are all one unit. Then, simply take the club back by turning your body. You should feel that your hands and wrists are doing nothing to manipulate the club.

This unified approach will help you get the club consistently on plane, which is the key to making consistent and optimum contact.

Top Notch

Achieving a solid "at the top" position is something every Tour player takes seriously. They don't all get to that position the same way, but they generally have a wide right elbow, a flexed right knee, and an upper body that's "stacked" above supporting legs. The following points are important:

❶ The hands should be well above the shoulders as the club reaches the top of the backswing, producing a wide arc.

❷ The right elbow should be clearly away from the body, which helps produce both leverage and power.

❸ The back should be facing the target as the hands reach the top of the backswing, indicating that you've made a full turn.

❹ Maintaining the flex in the right knee is absolutely critical—don't straighten the right leg at this point.

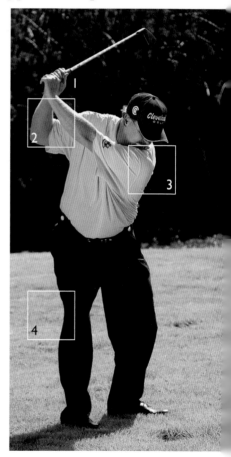

The best way to learn a proper "at the top" position is to continue the takeaway drill from page 21. From where the drill left off (**A**), simply raise up the club over your shoulder without manipulating it with your hands or wrists (**B**). At this point, your shoulders, hips, and knees have rotated as far as they have to. The clubshaft should be parallel to the target line, without pointing to either side. Achieving this position is essential for hitting the ball straight. A slightly cupped left wrist promotes a better striking of the ball.

A   **B**

On the Downswing

❶ As in the corresponding point in the takeaway, on the downswing the clubhead should be between the arms.

❷ The left arm must be almost perpendicular to the ground as the right forearm points at the ball. Keeping the left upper arm close to the chest is another hallmark of good players.

❸ The right leg has maintained its flex and has stayed back and away from the ball. Collapsing the right leg as you approach impact would prevent proper release and sap your swing's power.

❹ Notice how the back remains at the same angle it held at address. Maintaining this angle throughout the swing is a must.

One exercise to ingrain the proper downswing positions is the pump drill. Assume your normal setup position, and take the club up to the top of the swing (**A**). From there, slowly move the club to three-quarters down (**B**), and then to a position that's parallel to the ground (**C**). When you first try this, move the club as slowly as necessary in order to achieve the proper positions, and continue to pump the club in sets of three. As you feel more confident you're hitting the right spots, speed up the pumps until you're moving at the same rate as you would in a normal swing. As you perform this drill, be certain to keep your right hip back and away from the ball, and your right knee flexed.

A   **B**   **C**

At Impact

❶ The left side—including the shoulder, arm, hand, clubhead, and ball—should all be aligned. This is key for making solid impact.

❷ A flat left wrist at impact is a must for striking the ball crisply, whereas cupping the left wrist tends to produce weak shots.

❸ It is critical to transfer your weight largely onto the left foot. Hanging back will lead only to poor impact.

❹ To achieve more solidly compressed shots, the right shoulder should be a bit lower than the left.

To accustom yourself to feeling the proper impact position, begin by presetting your body and club at impact (**A**). Your right shoulder should be lower than the left, and your left shoulder, hip, arm, wrist, and hand should be aligned with both the clubshaft and the ball. Make sure your right hip has stayed back and that your right knee is slightly flexed. Also, to promote solid contact with the ball your left wrist should be flat and your weight should be shifted primarily to your left side. Once you achieve this position, take the club back slowly without swaying (**B**), then bring it down to the ball just hard enough to hit a chip shot (**C** and **D**). After some practice, you should be able consistently to reproduce this position naturally without having to preset your body or club.

Release

❶ A proper release always involves fully extending your arms and crossing them over one another. Full extension is a must for accuracy and power.

❷ The fingers of the left hand should be visible, indicating that the clubhead was square through impact.

❸ The left hip and leg should still be aligned in a straight line. This position is absolutely necessary if you want to strike the ball with authority. A firm left side also helps the club-head gain speed through impact.

❹ The right foot should remain on the ground until the power of the club swinging past the body pulls it up.

Although many amateur golfers struggle with their release, it really isn't that difficult to learn. Begin by assuming your normal address position, and then turn in your left foot (for a right-handed golfer) so that the toe is pointing away from the target (**A**). Next, pull your right foot well back of its normal position. Being careful to maintain this position, begin making abbreviated swings and concentrate on making solid contact with the ball. You should notice immediately that it's almost impossible to spin out with your shoulders or to swing over the top in an out-to-in pattern. Instead, you'll be forced to keep your front shoulder closed and your right hip back, away from the ball (**B**). The club should pass by your body rather easily, and the ball should travel significantly farther than you expect.

A　　　　　　　　　**B**

To the Finish

❶ A good, balanced finish should have the right shoulder positioned so that it's even or slightly ahead of the left foot.

❷ A straight back not only promotes good balance, but is much easier on your body than a reverse "C."

❸ The right foot should be pulled up into this position by the rotation of the body in the release.

❹ At the finish, the knees should be even with one another, indicating that you've turned fully, and your belt buckle should be facing the target.

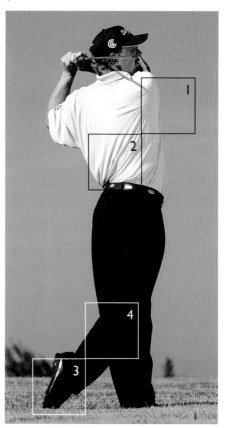

POWER DRILLS

Point Your Right Elbow

In the downswing, the left side leads while the right side supplies the power. It's like a one-two combination in boxing: Lead with the left jab, and follow with the right cross.

To get maximum power from your right side, it's critical to keep your right elbow pointed at your right hip. This is especially true as you enter the hitting area. This relationship between the right elbow and the right hip through the impact zone is one all good players share.

Take a few practice swings—maybe half or three-quarter ones—and concentrate on pointing your right elbow at your right hip. Practice your swing at home in front of a mirror to make this alignment second nature.

By keeping the right elbow in its proper position, you'll be able to fire from the right side while keeping a tight connection through impact. That will produce some big hits, or should we say, knockout shots?

Spin the Top

Golf is simple, if you'll only let it be. If you think about the swing at its most basic level, the game becomes child's play. All you have to do is spin the top.

When you spin a top, the string must be nice and tight. The same goes for the golf swing. When you take away the club, make sure you turn your shoulders, but keep your left hip where it was at address. This creates needed dynamic tension along your whole left side.

An easy way to create this dynamic tension while maintaining balance is to focus on your feet: Your weight should be distributed over the balls and heels. An easy way to guard against over-turning and sliding your hips on the backswing is to keep your front foot on the ground. Also, by not raising your left heel, you'll limit how much you can turn your hips.

Remember, you don't hit a golf ball with your backswing. If you lift your heel on the backswing, you turn your hips more easily, but you also dissipate the energy you're trying to store up for the downswing.

Throw the Flag

To guarantee a proper shoulder turn, practice by putting a towel in your right armpit at address (**A**). If the towel drops (**B**), you'll know you've stopped your shoulder turn too soon and swung to the top with your arms instead. This penalty flag that you're throwing on yourself will remind you to swing more with your body than with your arms.

A

B

Focus on the Finish

Many amateurs are so consumed with anxiety about the incremental parts of the swing (grip, alignment, posture, setup, etc.) that they lose sight of their overall objective, which is to strike the ball squarely and forcefully. One way to alleviate this anxiety is to focus on the finish.

Some of the benchmarks of the proper finish are as follow (and are shown on the opposite page):

❶ Good balance

❷ Weight forward on your left side

❸ Knees touching

❹ Belt buckle facing the target

❺ Club to the left of the left shoulder

❻ Right arm extended and right wrist flat

To get used to the feeling of a good finish position, start with the club at address and swing it forward to the finish. Hold that pose for several seconds, then repeat the address-to-finish move. Let your natural tempo dictate how slowly or quickly you swing the club.

If you understand where your swing needs to end up, you'll increase the likelihood of getting there.

Fight That Chicken Wing

Lack of extension is without doubt the biggest hindrance to power in golf. You don't have to be built like Tiger Woods to hit the ball long, but you do need to avoid the dreaded chicken wing (**A**). A bent front-arm position will sap power from even the strongest golfers.

To ensure a full extension, try this drill. Place a headcover under your front arm (the left arm for a right-handed golfer) (**B**) and begin taking full swings. The goal is to hold the headcover in place until the weight of the swinging club pulls your arms away from your body through impact (**C**). If you shorten your front arm (chicken wing), the headcover will fall out prematurely. By practicing this drill, you'll learn to achieve full extension and maximum power.

Ballflight Drills

Golfers are fascinated by ballflight. We all remember the thrill we felt when we first got the ball airborne. Most amateurs live for hitting towering shots that fly high and long. Better players, however, know that getting the ball high into the air isn't always a good thing. Although some professionals and seasoned amateurs are high-ball hitters, most produce a stronger, less dramatic ballflight, in which the ball powerfully flies off the clubface in a nice, gradual arc. This type of shot is less vulnerable to wind, is airborne longer off the tee, and is more consistently accurate on approaches to the green.

The following drills will help you develop the solid impact position that leads to a consistent ballflight that never gets boring.

Stop-at-Impact Drill

A mirror will help with this drill. Using a club but no ball, make a three-quarter swing at slightly slower than normal speed. Stop the swing at impact. Where is the club in relation to your body? Your weight should have moved to the left side, and your hands should be leading the clubhead. Your hips should be open to the target as well. Work on these points while you keep trying this drill. You'll know when you're getting it right, because everything—lower body, upper body, arms, hands, and club—will be swinging toward impact together.

Hit-the-Tee Drill

This drill promotes a "down and through" release. Place a tee in the ground at the point where you normally play the ball from your stance. Take a ball in your right hand, and set up as though you were going to hit a shot (**A**). Make a full swing motion (**B**). As you swing down, try to throw the ball at the tee (**C**). If you're like most players, you'll have some trouble at first, usually throwing the ball well out in front of the tee. Practice until you can consistently hit the area right around the tee. You'll then know what it means to release down into the ball.

A   **B**   **C**

Half-Swing Drill

With a five-iron, hit five shots at a target 100 yards away. What you want to do is to make a half-swing, taking your hands back no higher than shoulder level (**A**); then concentrate on making a good coordinated downswing with your hands and arms, with your upper and lower body working in unison (**B**). Make sure that you keep your hands firm through impact. Once you've got a feel for the 100-yard shot, gradually increase the length of the swing and the shot—-five balls at a time—to 125 yards, 150 yards, and then your full five-iron distance. Although the ball will fly higher for the longer shots, the gradual rising arc should remain the same.

Pivot for Proper Impact

An improper pivot is a common cause of poor ballstriking because it brings the low point of the swing too far behind the ball. To improve your pivot, try this "heel up" drill. Start by assuming the proper impact position, with your left hip slightly toward the target. Now lift your right heel off the ground. From this position, hit some short shots, and then gradually add power to your swing. This drill will help move the low point of your swing forward and induce a proper, descending hit on the ball.

THE SIX BAD SHOTS

An infinite number of things can go wrong in a full swing, but most of them result in one of six types of bad shots: hook, slice, push, pull, push-slice, and push-hook. For all of these, understanding the cause is essential to correcting the problem. In the following pages, we will address each of these faulty shots, and provide techniques that will help you avoid them.

Beat the Hook

It's been said that a hook is as close to a good golf shot as any. That's little comfort for the golfer who sees his shots curve dramatically toward a greenside bunker or water hazard.

A hook is generally the result of a sound swing path but a closed clubface, which imparts right-to-left sidespin at impact (for a right-handed golfer). The primary cause of a closed clubface is the clubhead passing the heads before striking the ball; it may also be the lower body sliding forward through impact rather than rotating, as shown below. When the lower body slides forward, the upper body hangs back, and the only way to make a proper release from this position is to flip the forearms and wrists—a move that shuts down the clubface.

Stand Firm

A good way to guard against lower-body slide (and the accompanying upper-body tilt to the right) is to swing next to a bag stand or similar object on the range. If you slide your hips on the downswing, you'll collide with the bag stand, as shown below. The only way to keep your lower body from hitting the stand is to rotate the hips. Implementing an aggressive hip turn will help keep your upper and lower body better connected and facilitate proper release.

Take Away Your Hook at the Start

Hook-swing flaws begin as early as on the takeaway. A common takeaway error is rolling the hands, which forces the clubface open and positions the clubhead behind the body (**A**). On the downswing after this start, your hand and arms must aggressively rotate the clubface to square it at impact; such exquisite timing is rare among amateurs, and more often the hands and arms will overrotate and close the face as it strikes the ball.

A quick fix for this is the ball pushback drill. Assume your normal address position, but with a ball placed a few inches behind the one you plan to strike (**B**). Take the club back straight away, making an effort to push back the second ball with the back of your clubhead (**C**). This straight path will bring you closer to eliminating that takeaway flaw.

B

C

Three-Ball Drill

Here's a way to become accustomed to the feeling of a more open clubface if you're used to shutting it down: Align three balls at a 45-degree angle in your setup. Address the ball closest to you (**A**), but attempt to hit the middle ball without striking the other two (**B**). To accomplish this, you'll have to carry your right shoulder higher through impact and maintain an open clubface. Both of these moves will help you fight your tendency to hook.

A   **B**

Equipment Tip

Many golfers don't realize that grips are offered in different thicknesses. If you have large hands and you're using standard-sized grips on your clubs, you're promoting too much hand action and risking premature closing of the clubface. Larger grips will help you take your hands out of the swing.

Slice Stoppers

A golf ball slices for two main reasons: either the clubface is open at impact, or the clubhead traces a path outside the target line and crosses to the inside through the impact zone with a face that's open relative to the path.

If you want to eliminate your slice rather than live with it, you must know where the clubhead is traveling in your golf swing and be able to control the clubface position throughout. The following drills will help you to develop your understanding and learn the proper positions. (For some ideas on how to live with your slice, refer to the advice on pages 18 and 19.)

Short-Shaft Yourself

Grip a club about 12 inches above the clubhead, and swing the club to the top of your backswing. The grip of the club should point directly at the target line, not inside or outside it (**A**). Then swing the club down so that the shaft lines up with your left arm and the clubface is square at the impact position. Focus on getting the clubshaft and left arm to form one straight line at impact (**B**).

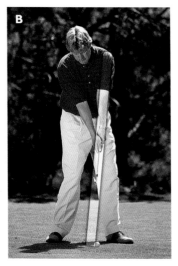

The Toe Knows

Practice hitting balls from an address position that lines up the ball with the toe of the club (**C**). This will help you remember to rotate the clubhead to a squared position as it moves through the impact zone.

Heels for Balance

Place your heels about three inches apart and point your toes outward. Assume your normal posture, with the ball off your left heel, and make a balanced golf swing. The purpose of this drill is to let the hands swing the club while the body follows through with the motion. Golfers who tend to turn their bodies before they drop their hands leave the clubface open at impact, causing a slice. Make sure you finish with your hips and back foot facing the target. Focusing on the hands swinging the clubhead will teach you how to improve your balance, tempo, pivot, and path.

Split Hands for Release

Grip the club with your hands split apart about three to four inches. Swing the club back, with an emphasis on keeping it on the proper path. On the downswing, focus on releasing the club so that it points straight down at impact and then out toward the target at the beginning of the follow-through. Splitting apart your hands will promote a proper release that causes the clubface to be square at impact.

Thumbing It

Assume your address position, and swing the club to hip-height, or until your left hand has extended to shake hands with an imaginary person on your right. The left thumb should point parallel to your target line (**A**).

Now, swing to impact. Focus on pointing both thumbs down at the ball as contact is made (**B**). This will help you learn to square the clubface at impact. In the hip-high follow-through, the right thumb should extend to a mirrored hand-shake position, with your hips facing the target and the shaft lying parallel to the target line (**C**).

By focusing on how your thumbs and hands move, you'll gain better control of the clubface throughout the swing.

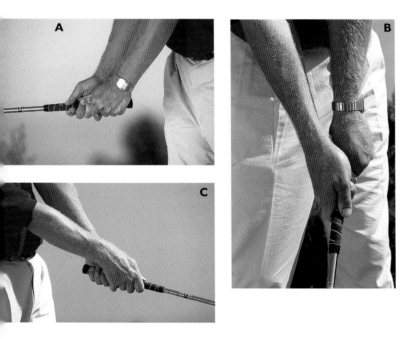

Push Comes to Shove

A pushed shot won't ruin your game unless it finds the right-hand rough. Unlike a hook or slice, which is caused by pure clubface errors, a push is a result of swing-path flaws. Typically, the path is too far inside-out and the clubface is square in relation to the swing plane.

A common fault that causes pushed shots is laying off the club at the top of the backswing, where the shaft rests below the desired swing plane (**A**). You can correct this fault by improving your takeaway. Take your stance on a concrete or tiled patio or sidewalk, with your toes lined up on a seam or groove in the flooring (**B** and **C**). Bring the club back waist-high; the shaft should be parallel to the ground, and if you look back at it, the shaft should cover your view of the seam in the floor.

A   **B**   **C**

Fighting a Pull

Pull swings typically result in long, powerful shots, often in the direction you'd rather they not go. Pulls are the result of square ball/clubface contact and a swing path that's too far outside-in (**A**). The usual cause is a downswing initiated by the shoulders. If the shoulders begin rotating too early, they force the club onto an outside-in plane.

A unique drill that helps eliminate early shoulder spin is the One-Foot Drill. Take your address position with your feet together, then drop your rear foot back. Raise the heel of that back foot until you're balanced on your front foot and back toe (**B**). Begin making full swings. If you spin your shoulders to start the downswing, you'll throw yourself off balance. Once you're able to make consistent contact with the ball, you'll know your keeping your shoulder movements to a minimum during the transition.

The Dreaded Push-Slice

Shots that start right and keep veering right are no fun and seem always to go awry. They result from a combination of clubface and swing-path errors: the face being open to the target line and the club being swung on an inside-out path.

A faulty backswing is more often than not the culprit in the push-slice. Many amateurs take the club too far back to the inside. When the club gets behind you, it's easy to let the hips and legs slide and wind up in a reverse pivot at the top (**A**). From this position, the only way to get the club back toward the ball is to drop the right shoulder on the downswing, moving the club onto an excessive inside-out path (the push) while causing the clubface to open (the slice). This combination of errors is often called "Rock and Block."

One of the easiest ways to guard against a takeaway that's too far inside is to concentrate on keeping the "Y" formed by the clubshaft and your arms intact throughout. This keeps the clubshaft on plane, correcting the biggest error in this perennial round-buster (**B**).

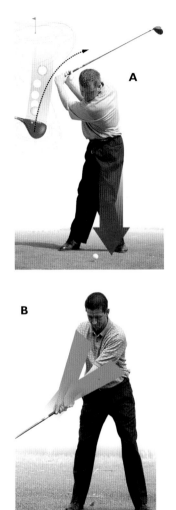

Stop the Push-Hook

The push-hook doesn't yield the disastrous effects of some other ballflights, yet it still involves both clubface and path errors; that is, the face is closed while the path is too far inside-out. The primary cause is rooted in the setup. Many golfers get in the habit of playing the ball too far back in the stance, especially those who play frequently in windy conditions. These players also tend to use a strong right-handed grip; this combination will typically result in the push-hook.

To fix your inside-out path, practice swinging with the intention of driving the butt end of the grip toward the inside of your front knee. This will help keep the club-shaft in front of your body, leading to a more down-the-line swing path.

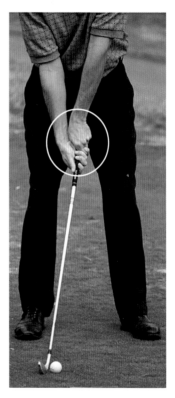

The Short Game and Putting

If you're like most golfers, at least half your shots are executed from within fifty yards of the hole. And, you also spend the vast majority of your practice time on the range, taking full swings.

The fastest route to lower scores is turning three shots into two around the greens. Technique and touch are the keys to a sounder short game. Although there's no substitute for time spent on the little shots, time spent repeating the improper techniques will establish flaws instead of improving results. The drills that follow will give you a firm grounding in the basics of the short game, and take the fear out of playing close.

OUT OF THE BUNKER EVERY TIME

Although the bunker shot is one of the easiest plays in golf, many amateurs still struggle with it. They don't understand that to make solid bunker shots, you have to strike the sand, not the ball. Because of this, there's a more generous margin for error on a bunker shot than there is from the fairway, where contact must be precise. From the bunker, you want to toss out a handful of sand with the swing; because the ball is the biggest "grain of sand" in the handful, it will go the farthest.

A good drill for accomplishing this is to draw a line in the sand about two inches behind the ball, and practice slapping that line with the sole of your club as you swing through. Once you can do this consistently, your bunker play will improve dramatically.

PITCH IT CLOSE

Crisp pitching requires an abrupt takeaway and a relatively steep downswing. If your problem is that you scoop the ball instead of hitting down on it, try this drill: Place a headcover a couple of feet behind the ball at setup (**A**). Practice taking your backswing without making contact with the headcover (**B** and **C**). Doing so will force the desired takeaway and lead to a steep downswing for better contact and increased spin.

A

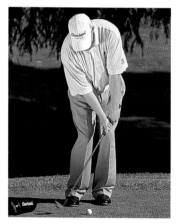

B

C

CHIN UP

When you're executing short-game shots, it's absolutely critical for you to be able to slide the leading edge of the club under the ball. The only way to slide the club effectively is to give your arms plenty of room to swing. To do this, you must stand tall and keep your head up (**A, B,** and **C**); otherwise, it's easy to skull the shot over the green or chunk it short of the target.

A

B

C

BRUSH THE GRASS

A great way to develop more confidence on those tricky in-between shots, as in this pitch over a bunker, is to coordinate your eyes and body. Instead of simply guessing how hard to swing, focus on the target and swing the club through the grass while trying to gauge the distance. Move the club back and forth. Then step up to the ball and play the shot. Your eyes and body know more than you think, if only you'll pay attention to them.

LAG WITH TEMPO

Many players on Tour practice with a metronome (available at most music stores) to hone their distance control on the greens and to match the timing of their stroke to an even beat. Remember, you want a constant tempo, whether the putt is three feet or thirty feet long; the only difference is how far you take the putterhead back and through.

Practice putts of varying lengths. Concentrate on your tempo by matching the timing of your stroke with that of the metronome. As you move between distances, take stock of how far back you need to position your putter to roll the ball the appropriate length. Make mental notes of specific stroke lengths so you can refer back to them when faced with similar-length putts on the course.

STEP-BY-STEP PROGRAMMING

To be a good lag putter, you have to be able to judge distances accurately. Stepping off your putts during a round is a good way to program your internal distance computer. It's also essential for your practice routine.

On the putting green, place a few balls at different distances from the fringe. Pace off the distance from each group, and try to stroke the ball right to the edge of the fringe. Putting to the fringe instead of to the hole will keep you from focusing too much on the specific line; the purpose here is to hone your feeling for distance. Then, when you face a putt of similar length on the course—which you'll recognize because you'll pace it off—you'll know just how to lag it close.

PUTTING WITH YOUR EYES CLOSED

Another solid drill for distance control is to practice putting with your eyes closed. Blind putting forces you to visualize the stroke and keeps you from becoming too wedded to the line instead of the distance. More three-putts result from being too short or too long than from being too far left or far right.

LOOK BEFORE YOU LAG

When you toss a ball at a target, do you look at the target while you throw, or do you stare at the ball and try to guide your hand along? You look at the target, of course; otherwise, you'd be lucky to get the ball out of your own shadow.

Inconsistent lag putting can result from focusing too much on the ball instead of on the target. Try setting up to the ball and starting to concentrate on the hole while you're making your practice strokes. Then hit the putt without taking your eyes off the hole or looking down at the ball.

STROKE IT WELL

Many amateurs faced with a long putt think they really have to smack it to get it to the hole. Although coming up way short will do you no good, thinking you must hit it hard may make you use your wrist too much in your putting stroke. A long putting stroke must be generated by the shoulders, not the wrists. So instead of thinking about hitting it hard, fix your thoughts on "stroking it well."

HOLD THAT LINE

Golfers miss short putts typically because of a putting stroke that travels inside or outside the target line. If you're missing more than your share of short putts, get yourself back on track by using four tees and two pieces of string. Construct a pathway that runs straight, no more than five or six feet in length, and only slightly wider than your putterhead. Then take your stroke, and concentrate on keeping the putter within the track as you swing it back and through. Repetition will give you the confidence you need out on the course.

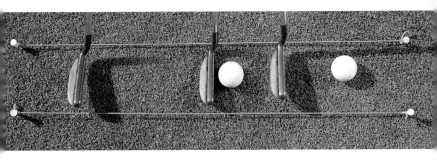

FIXES

On the Tee

The first shot of the hole sets the agenda for everything that follows. It's usually the shot that travels farthest, and it's also the shot that can go awry the most. Many of the developments in equipment have aimed at making drivers more forgiving and adding distance. These clubs allow you to hit the ball farther with less effort, which lets you concentrate on developing your accuracy off the tee. You'll hit more greens with a five-iron from the fairway than you will with a seven-iron from the rough (or anything from the trees). The tips that follow are concerned mostly with helping you straighten yourself out when your drive goes astray.

DEVELOPING A PRESHOT ROUTINE

A good way to increase your consistency is to develop your own preshot routine and to use it every time. Preshot routines vary from golfer to golfer, and it doesn't necessarily matter what you do in the moments leading up to the address, as long as you do the same thing before every shot.

Tour pro Skip Kendall starts by selecting his club, then takes several practice swings behind the ball, emphasizing whatever his swing key is at the time. Then he selects his target from behind the ball and visualizes the kind of shot he wants to hit. This step contains much of the mental work that leads to accurate driving: to eliminate all negative thoughts, focus on your target, and simply "let it go."

DRIVING WITHOUT A DRIVER

Having trouble hitting fairways with your driver? Because it's the longest and least lofted club in the bag (excluding putters), it's also the most difficult to control. This is true for pros as well as amateurs; think of how many Tour pros opt for three-woods or even long irons on tight driving holes. If the world's best golfers feel the need to hit with something other than a driver when the target seems small, you should feel no shame about doing the same. A reliable club that puts you on the short grass is your best friend on the tee.

ADDRESSING YOUR ADDRESS

An accurate driver swing is all about balance, control, and coordination. These qualities all start at the address, where your stance should be shoulder-width and your feet flared to facilitate your turn. The right shoulder should hang slightly lower than the left. When the right shoulder is positioned lower, it makes it much easier to swing on the preferred outside-to-inside path.

Fight the urge to play the ball too far forward or too far back in your stance. Typically, if you play the ball too far forward, you'll encourage a pull, whereas playing it too far back will encourage a push. Use a neutral position, playing the ball off your shirt logo.

BEING TEE SMART

Most amateurs walk unthinkingly to the middle of the tee box and place their peg in the ground in the first grassy spot they find. But good strategy can come into play even in matters as small as the place between the markers you start from.

If there's trouble on the left side of the hole, then starting from the extreme left of the tee box lets you aim away from the danger. If you play a fade, starting on the right side of the box gives your ball more room to come back to the fairway. In windy conditions, you probably want to play into the wind rather than against it, so if the wind is blowing left-to-right, set up on the left side.

Playing the angles is the easiest form of smart golf imaginable. It's the one time you get to pick your spot: use it to your advantage.

SEQUENCE FOR POWER

Of the many errors golfers make when trying to swing for the fences, the most damaging is swinging the right shoulder, from the top, across the target line. This malady stems from a false belief that in order to hit the ball hard, you have to hit it with your right side. It can also result from rotating too quickly on the downswing or, more specifically, rotating out of sequence. By that, we mean that the shoulders turn faster than the hips. To create maximum power, your turning sequence should be as follows: hips, shoulders, hands.

The best way to keep from coming over the top and swinging out of sequence is to set up with your right arm positioned inside your left. When you do, you'll establish a power-rich swing plane and keep that right shoulder from swinging out of turn.

A SLICE FIX IS IN YOUR HANDS

For a quick way to prevent slicing the ball when you swing, try strengthening your grip by rotating your hands clockwise (to your right for a right-handed golfer). Most amateurs have a tough time squaring the clubface through the hitting zone, and a strong grip can help achieve a square or even slightly closed clubface at impact. A stronger grip will both fight the slice and promote crisper contact.

Full-Swing Fixes

There's no substitute for a sound full swing; the fundamentals on pages 20–30 are the key to developing a repetitive, accurate, powerful motion to the ball and through the swing. The Fixes that follow will touch on techniques for some of the most difficult shots you'll face in a round; these tips are first aid for the most common problems, letting you get back to the clubhouse in one piece until you can give the fault your full attention.

ADJUSTMENTS

Square at the Top for Straighter Shots

To hit the ball straight, you have to square the clubface at the top of your backswing. If the face is closed, you'll most likely hit a smoother hook; an open face will result in severe slices.

A quick way to be sure you're squaring the clubface at the top is to concentrate on feeling most of the club's weight in your left thumb at the top. When the face is too open or too closed, it's usually because the hands are rotated in the wrong direction. However, when your left thumb is under the club, you know that your clubface is square.

"Sweep Down" on Fairway Woods

There are a lot of frustrating things in golf, but near the top of the list is failing to capitalize on a perfectly struck tee shot by topping your second shot fifty yards down the fairway with a wood. Golfers struggle to hit the ball solidly from the fairway with their woods because they've been told to "sweep" them like a tee shot.

It's okay to describe the fairway wood swing as a sweeping motion (**A**), but don't confuse "sweep" with "swing up,"

which works for tee shots because the ball is forward and raised. The correct approach isn't much different than it is with a long iron. First position the ball opposite the logo on your shirt (about an inch behind where you'd set up to hit a driver); then, use a neutral hand position that is even with the ball (resist the temptation to forward press) (**B**) and swing down and through the shot to a full, balanced finish, letting the club work its way into the grass and taking a slight divot just after striking the ball. You will build up speed throughout the shot, and the longer shaft will provide increased clubhead speed for extra distance.

Fairway Woods from Moderate Rough

As long as half the ball is above the top of the grass (**A**), you can play a full shot with a wood—especially the utility woods of today. Five-, seven-, and nine-woods all deliver the distance of long irons, but their lower centers of gravity and wide surface area at the sole will displace more of the grass and let you make solid contact.

To prevent the long grass from dissipating the clubhead's energy, you must hit this shot with a more descending blow than from the fairway. Grip the handle an inch or so farther down and stand a bit closer to the ball to encourage a steeper angle on the forward swing. Taking a more vertical back-swing will also ensure the best angle of attack for this shot (**B**). Try to take a divot; this will get you working down into the ball, maximizing the loft of the wood by making contact in the middle of the clubface. The ball should come out with a higher trajectory than with a long iron, but without sacrificing any distance.

A

Bunker Woods

Under the right conditions, a utility wood can be a great choice for a long fairway bunker shot. Lofted woods are much easier to hit with from sand than long irons, since the former's soleplate gives excellent protection against digging into the sand.

The time to use this shot is when the ball is sitting up on relatively firm sand, and the loft of the wood is sufficient to get over the lip of the bunker.

Start by gripping down an inch on the club, which will help keep you from digging into the sand. Widen your stance to create a stable base, and restrict the movement of your legs and hips to encourage solid contact. Play the ball more toward the middle of your stance, since it is essential that you strike the ball before the sand. Dig your feet into the sand just a little bit, to avoid lowering the bottom of your swing. Make a three-quarters armswing back, and swing through to a balanced finish. Solid contact is the goal; distance will take care of itself.

Cheat the Wind

Hitting an iron shot into the wind from a tightly mowed fairway can be tough. However, with the proper technique, it becomes relatively simple. Start by placing the ball well back in your stance to promote solid contact. Depending on the wind, you'll want to hit at least one, if not two or three clubs more than normal (which will also help keep the ball low). Concentrate on a slow, smooth takeaway and try to return the club to the address position. After some practice, you'll be surprised how easily and consistently this shot bores through the wind.

Tree Trouble

A trouble shot that presents unique difficulties arises when your ball comes to rest next to a tree, so that you'd have to hit it backhanded to make contact. While that's one possible solution (albeit difficult to pull off), another way to handle the situation is to turn your iron so that the toe is pointing down and then to hit the shot left-handed (for a right-handed golfer).

To execute this shot, take a seven- or eight-iron and assume a lefty stance (**A**). You can use either a cross-handed or left grip, although it's easier for most people to use the latter. Grip down on the club to get better control, and take a short punch swing with little or no wrist cock (**B**).

When attempting this shot, it's crucial to keep your head steady because holding the club in such an unfamiliar fashion will make it impossible for you to adjust for any lateral swaying during the swing. First take a number of practice swings so you can get an idea of what the shot will feel like. Don't get too ambitious with the shot: Your goal is to get it back in play, not to pull off a miracle that lands you on the green.

Quick Fix: Pulls

Taking the club away to the inside forces the golfer to "loop" the club at the top of the swing and come across the ball at impact, resulting in a pull when the clubface is square. Avoid the loop by taking the clubhead straight back. Place a golf club a few inches behind your ball along the target line. During the takeaway, your club should pass over the length of the grip of the club on the ground before making its way skyward.

Arms, Then Shoulders

The upper body and arms play separate roles in the swing. When a ball is pushed, it is often because these roles have been reversed. In a fundamentally sound swing, the arms initiate the downswing. Once the arms are on their path downward, then you allow your body to turn. Remember, first arms down, then upper body around.

Quick Fix: Pushes

Many pushers of the ball align left of where they think they are aiming. If you're aligned left of your target, you'll naturally swing along an inside-out path because your body will swing the clubhead toward where your mind is telling it to go. To straighten out your alignment, point the clubface at the target first; then align your shoulders, hips, and feet parallel to the clubface.

SLICE STOPPERS

Check Your Grip

A

You can greatly increase your chance of squaring the club at impact if you grip the club properly. It helps to grip the club with your left hand by your left side instead of out in front of you (**A**). You want to set the grip in your fingers to match the angle of the shaft. The key is to place the heel pad of your left hand on top of the grip, so that your wrist will be on top of the grip as well (**B**). Tap the ground a few times to get a feel for how the left wrist hinges.

Now move the club in front of you and notice how the left hand is slightly bent at the wrist and how the "V" formed by your thumb and index finger points at your right shoulder. Wrap your right-hand fingers around the underside of the grip, and mold the hollow of your right palm over your left thumb. The "V" formed by the right thumb and index finger should point to your right shoulder as well.

Let the Clubhead Win

To decrease the amount of sidespin you put on your shots, picture your clubhead coming from an inside-out path and reaching the finish line—your left toe—first. Your hands should finish second, and your shoulders should bring up the rear. Remember, once your hands reach the finish line, extend the clubhead out to the target in the follow-through.

Line It Up

Slicers usually compensate for their tendency to slice by subconsciously aiming left of their target, typically by flaring open the front foot and opening their body lines (**A**). Unfortunately, aligning yourself in such a fashion accentuates several flaws associated with slicing. Instead, work on aligning yourself squarely with your target; you can incorporate a flared right foot, but make sure your shoulders are parallel to an imaginary line that runs from the ball to your target.

Head Trip

Amateurs are often told to "keep their head over the ball." The problem with this advice is that it often forces a player to plant his or her weight on the front foot (**B**). This reverse-pivot position typically results in an open clubface at impact and hence, a slice. Instead, set up with your head a little bit behind the ball, and don't fixate on keeping it in place.

Feel the Weight

One reason for the open clubface that causes a slice may be the golfer's lack of awareness of the clubhead's location during the swing. In order to control the clubface, you have to have a strong sense of its position. Most amateurs grip the club far too tightly, and therefore never "feel" its weight. Get a better sense of the clubhead by holding the club before address at a 45-degree angle in front of you with a lighter than normal grip. Waggle the club and focus on its balance and weight. When you've committed that feel to memory, you'll be better able to control the position of the clubface throughout the swing.

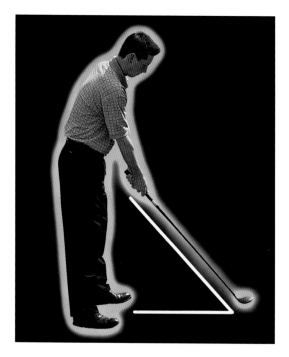

Short-Game Fixes

The short game leaves the most room for creativity. The shots you will face have a number of possible solutions, and choosing the best one will require that you understand the conditions both on the ground and in the air, as well as your own degree of comfort with the various options. Generally speaking, safest is best, but no matter how much you'd rather chip than pitch, sometimes you will be confronting a shot over a bunker and have no choice but to pitch. Use these tips to get you through the variety of situations you'll face in every round.

TOSS YOUR PITCHES

If you're confused about the amount of body action to use on a pitch shot, imagine pitching horseshoes. In this underhanded motion, the arms and body work together in response to the target; the body parts aren't consciously controlled, but react naturally to the task at hand. Focusing on your target will do the same thing for your pitch shots. If you're pitching the ball onto the front edge of the green, imagine the landing area as the stake, and throw a ringer.

WHEN YOU'RE IN DEEP

Club selection is always crucial in sand play, yet it's often overlooked. When you're in a deep bunker, a lofted wedge—like a 60-degree model—is a must. Set up with an open clubface and the majority of your weight planted on your front foot (**A**). Since you'll need some power to get the ball airborne, this shot requires a full swing with a fair amount of speed through impact (**B**). Don't be afraid to give it a good whack—it's unlikely that a properly struck shot will travel too far.

BUNKER HIGHS AND LOWS

When you're in a greenside bunker, you have options, just as you have in any short-game shot. You can play the shot either high or low, depending on the depth of the bunker and the distance to the pin.

For a low, running bunker shot (perfect for shallow bunkers and when there's plenty of distance between you and the pin), keep the clubface square at impact and finish with a low follow-through (**A**). Be sure to allow for plenty of roll once the ball lands on the green.

A

For a high bunker shot (perfect for greenside pot bunkers or if there's little room between you and pin), open the clubface and aim it at your landing area, while you point your feet well left of the target (**B**). Take a longer backswing, and allow the club to pull your arms into a nice, high finish (**C**). The ball will come out at a steep angle and should land softly.

B   **C**

SAND-SLOPE BASICS

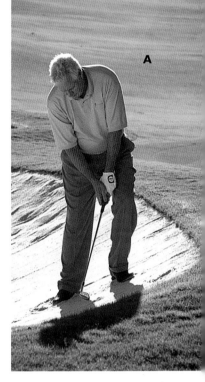

The sand is truly nothing to fear. If you learn the proper techniques and practice them, almost any sand shot can be executed with relative ease.

For example, the uphill bunker shot isn't nearly as difficult as most golfers believe (although strength is very helpful in executing it). Simply position the ball near your front foot, with most of your weight on that foot (**A**). Close the clubface (yes, close it) and take a full swing. However, you won't be able to make a complete follow-through because of the uphill stance, so be prepared.

The downhill bunker shot is one of the most challenging in golf. Use a lob wedge for short shots and a sand wedge for longer shots; the slope will effectively reduce the loft of the club. Take your normal address position; then widen your stance several inches and flare out your front foot at least 45 degrees. Your body should be aimed left of the target, and the ball should be played off your front foot (**B**). Adjust your shoulders to match the slope, which will steepen the plane and ensure that you hit the sand approximately two to three inches behind the ball. On the backswing, turn your shoulders first and then swing the club to the top. As you do, fold your right elbow and hinge your wrists as soon as possible to create a more vertical plane (**C**). Make sure you maintain your wrist hinge as you start swinging down; at impact, you want to swing down into the sand without flipping your club at the ball. The ball will fly lower than normal; if there's a steep bank in front of you, you may have to aim away from it.

On the downhill shot, it's best to be prudent and to know your limitations; if the slope is too steep, or you don't feel confident, you may be better off going out of the bunker sideways, or even backwards. The pros make all these shots look easy because they practice them every day. If you work on them at least a couple of times a month, you'll also see positive results.

B   C

LONG BUNKER SHOTS

The mistake most golfers make when attempting a long bunker shot is miscalculating how far they can hit the ball. If you can hit your sand wedge sixty yards off the fairway, you'll probably hit it only thirty yards out of the sand. In light of this fact, try hitting this shot with your pitching wedge, or even with a nine- or eight-iron. These clubs are particularly useful when you're in a bunker and have to clear another bunker before reaching the green.

PUTT IT OUT

Never mind what your partners will say. If the sand is firm, your lie is good, and there's no lip to contend with, your best option from the bunker may be to putt it out. Just assume your normal putting grip and stance, remembering not to ground your club. Then try to make contact with the equator of the ball—it's important to give it overspin if you're going to get safely out of the trap and onto the green.

PUTTER BLAST

A very different type of bunker shot can also be played with a putter—and probably cannot be played effectively with anything else. If your ball is buried in the face of a bunker, using a wedge often only forces the ball deeper into the sand. But if you turn your putter counterclockwise so that the toe is pointing toward the ball (**A**), you may be able to blast it out in an unexpected way.

Set up with the ball in the middle to front of your stance, and assume a normal, full-swing grip. Take up the club abruptly, and come down with a limited follow-through, as you would when hitting a punch shot (**B**). If you make contact with the sand behind the ball, it should come out like a normal bunker shot.

This technique works best with heel-toe-style putters.

A

B

COLLARED GREENS

A common trouble shot most golfers face comes when, after making an approach shot to the green, the ball comes to rest against the collar where the green or fringe and the first cut of rough meet. It is difficult to get the putter on the ball cleanly, and there's no way to chip effectively on account of the grass behind the ball.

Your best option in this situation is to putt with your sand wedge by matching up the equator (centerline) of the ball with the leading edge of the blade. Grip down on the club as far as necessary to reach a comfortable address position, and use your normal putting stroke. You'll know you've executed the shot correctly if the ball comes out rolling end-over-end like a putt.

FAIRWAY WOOD CHIPS

Everyone has seen this shot made by Tiger Woods, but it doesn't take Tiger's skills to pull it off. A fairway wood is appropriate for chipping when your ball comes to rest in fluffy grass, but is sitting up enough to make accurate chipping with a wedge problematic. It's also a good option whenever you have a fair amount of green to work with, or when there are several feet of rough between the ball and the green.

Grip down on the club far enough to be comfortable, and don't be concerned if you have to go down to the end of the grip. Use your normal chipping grip, but make less of an up-and-down stroke than you would with a wedge. Keep in mind that this shot isn't designed to "bite" when it reaches the green, but rather to stay low to the ground and to roll almost like a putt. As long as you've got plenty of green between you and the hole, you'll find this to be an effective tool in your greenside arsenal.

LOB OR RUN?

To hit a high pitch (**A** and **B**), select a lofted wedge and position the ball slightly forward in your stance. A high, balanced finish will allow you to carry the ball well onto the green. To play the low shot (**C** and **D**), position the ball back in your stance and use a less lofted club. Finish with your hands relatively low, and let the ball roll all the way to the hole.

A   **B**

Which is the better option for you? For most people, and for most of the time, it's the low shot rather than the high pitch. You have to land both of them accurately, but the lower one will land much closer to you and run from there. It's also a safer shot with less risk of mis-hitting. If there are no hazards or long grass between you and the green, the low shot is the way to go.

C   D

THE UNDERREACH

When it comes to the short game, the biggest problem recreational golfers have is chunked shots. To help prevent fat chips and pitches, try the underreach technique. Begin by assuming your address position, with your arms hanging at their natural length. Choke down on the club about an inch, and hover it just off the ground as you get ready to execute the shot. The combination of choking the grip and hovering the club will help you guard against making a fat shot. When you finally do make a swing, simply concentrate on hitting the bottom half of the ball.

BOOK YOUR GRIP

Consistent grip pressure during the putting stroke is crucial. One way to help maintain it is to learn to create equal inward force in both hands. On the takeaway, the top hand should apply pressure towards the bottom hand, and the reverse is true on the forward stroke.

To get a feel for this equal pressure, imagine that you're swinging a book rather than a putter. In order to make a full stroke without dropping the book, you'll have to apply equal and controlled pressure in both directions, with your wrists passively going along for the ride. Learn to recognize this sensation, and your putting stroke will improve dramatically.

Index

Acknowledgments

Special thanks to the *Golf Tips*® Instruction Panel:

Senior Instruction Editors

Glenn Deck, Glenn Deck Golf Academy at Pelican Hill Resort

Carl Rabito, Rabito Golf Schools

Brady Riggs, Woodley Lakes Golf Course

Marshall Smith, Peoria Ridge Golf Club

Todd Sones, Todd Sones Impact Golf

Joe Thiel, World Wide Golf Schools

T.J. Tomasi, Ph.D., Lyman Orchards Golf Club

Chuck Winstead, English Turn Golf and Country Club

Instruction Editors

A.J. Bonar, AJ Golf School

Mike Clinton, GolfTEC

Jerry Elwell, Max Out Golf

Craig Farnsworth, D.O., See and Score Golf School

Steve Mitchell, Kiawah Island Resort

Karen Palacios-Jansen, Swing Blade Golf

Dan Pasquariello, Pebble Beach Golf Academy

Jeff Ritter, ASU Karsten Golf Academy

Art Sellinger, TPC at Las Colinas

Laird Small, Pebble Beach Golf Academy

Mel Sole, Phil Ritson-Mel Sole Golf Schools

Tom Stickney, The Club at Cordillera